Exploring How To Get The Deal That You Want In A Negotiation

How To Develop The Skill Of Exploring What Is Possible In A Negotiation In Order To Reach The Best Possible Deal

"Practical, proven techniques that will help you get the best deal possible out of your next negotiation"

Dr. Jim Anderson

Published by:
Blue Elephant Consulting
Tampa, Florida

Printed in the United States of America

Library of Congress Control Number: 2016919804

ISBN-13: 978-1540690029

ISBN-10: 1540690024

Warning – Disclaimer

The purpose of this book is to educate and entertain. This book does not promise or guarantee that anyone following the ideas, tips, suggestions, techniques or strategies will be successful. The author, publisher and distributor(s) shall have neither liability nor responsibility to anyone with respect to any loss or damage caused, or alleged to be caused, directly or indirectly by the information contained in this book.

<u>Recent Books By The Author</u>

<u>Product Management</u>

- How Product Managers Can Sell More Of Their Product: Tips & Techniques For Product Managers To Better Understand How To Sell Their Product

- Product Development Lessons For Product Managers: How Product Managers Can Create Successful Products

<u>Public Speaking</u>

- Changing How You Speak To Overcome Your Fear Of Speaking: Change techniques that will transform a speech into a memorable event

- Delivering Excellence: How To Give Presentations That Make A Difference: Presentation techniques that will transform a speech into a memorable event

<u>CIO Skills</u>

- Keeping The Barbarians Out: How CIOs Can Secure Their Department and Company: Tips And Techniques For CIOs To Use In Order To Secure Both Their IT Department And Their Company

- What CIOs Need To Know In Order To Successfully Manage An IT Department: Decision Making Skills That Every CIO Needs To Have In Order To Be Able To Make The Right Choices

- How CIOs Can Make Innovation Happen: Tips And Techniques For CIOs To Use In Order To Make Innovation Happen In Their IT Department

IT Manager Skills

- How To Build High Performance IT Teams: Tips And Techniques That IT Managers Can Use In Order To Develop Productive Teams

- Building The Perfect Team: What Staffing Skills Do IT Managers Need?: Tips And Techniques That IT Managers Can Use In Order To Correctly Staff Their Teams

- Secrets Of Effective Leadership For IT Managers: Tips And Techniques That IT Managers Can Use In Order To Develop Leadership Skills

Negotiating

- Use The Power Of Arguing To Win Your Next Negotiation: How To Develop The Skill Of Effective Arguing In A Negotiation In Order To Get The Best Possible Outcome

- Learn How To Signal In Your Next Negotiation: How To Develop The Skill Of Effective Signaling In A Negotiation In Order To Get The Best Possible Outcome

Miscellaneous

- How To Heal A Broken Leg – Fast!: Understanding how to deal with a broken leg in order to start walking again quickly

- How Software Defined Networking (SDN) Is Going To Change Your World Forever: The Revolution In Network Design And How It Affects

Note: See a complete list of books by Dr. Jim Anderson at the back of this book.

Acknowledgements

Any book like this one is the result of years of real-world work experience. In my over 25 years of working for 7 different firms, I have met countless fantastic people and I've been mentored by some truly exceptional ones. Although I've probably forgotten some of the people who made me the person that I am today, here is my attempt to finally give them the recognition that they so truly deserve:

- Thomas P. Anderson
- Art Puett
- Bobbi Marshall
- Bob Boggs

Dr. Jim Anderson

This book is dedicated to my wife Lori. None of this would have been possible without her love and support.

Thanks for the best 21 years of my life (so far)...!

Speaking.   Negotiating.   Managing.   Marketing.

Table Of Contents

Learn To Explore In Order To Get The Deal That You Want

When we enter into a negotiation, we simply don't know everything that we need to know. What this means for us is that we've got to use the negotiation to do some exploring – we've got to get answers to the questions that are unanswered when we start.

In order to accomplish this we're going to have to make sure that we have the time that we need to think about what the other side is telling us. When they hit us with a lot of facts and stats to back up their position, we need to take the time to understand where all of these numbers came from.

In order to get the deal that we want, we're going to have to give in on some of the issues that are being discussed. What issues we make concessions on and how we go about making those concessions is very important. Done correctly, we'll get closer to the deal that we want.

In order to get better at this negotiating thing, we need to understand how to use all of the tools that are available to us. This includes the telephone. Additionally, it sure would be nice if we could get some professional negotiators to share with us how they have become so successful.

One of the things that we need to be aware of during a negotiation is that we can't always trust what the other side is telling us. We need to learn to not believe the other side. This also means that we should get some guidance from someone who has done all of this before.

Although it's not a word that a lot of us use very often, haggling is a critical part of any negotiation. We need to learn what it is and how to do it. The more that you talk with the other side, the better your chances of learning what their hidden needs are.

A negotiation can take some time to complete. This means that as negotiators we need to learn how to be persistent in order to get what we want. We may not have the best product, the best price, or be the most competitive but we can still walk away with the deal that we want.

For more information on what it takes to be a great negotiator, check out my blog, The Accidental Negotiator, at:

www.TheAccidentalNegotiator.com

Good luck!

- Dr. Jim Anderson

About The Author

I must confess that I never set out to be a negotiator. When I went to school, I studied Computer Science and thought that I'd get a nice job programming and that would be that. Well, at least part of that plan worked out!

My first job was working for Boeing on their F/A-18 fighter jet program. I spent my days programming fighter jet software in assembly language and I loved it. The U.S. government decided to save some money and went looking for other countries to sell this plane to. This put me into an unfamiliar role: I started to negotiate with foreign military officials and I ended up having to participate in the negotiations for large international deals.

Time moved on and so did I. I found myself working for Siemens, the big German telecommunications company. They were making phone switches and selling them to the seven U.S. phone companies. The problem was that the switches were too complicated. When it came time to negotiate a deal with the customer, the sales teams struggled to create an effective negotiating strategy. I was called in to bridge the world between the product functionality and the business impacts as they related to the negotiations.

I've spent over 25 years working as a negotiator for both big companies and startups. This has given me an opportunity to learn what it takes to both plan and execute negotiations of all sizes. When it comes to negotiations, I've pretty much been there, done that.

I now live in Tampa Florida where I spend my time managing my consulting business, Blue Elephant Consulting, teaching college courses at the University of South Florida, and traveling to work with companies like yours to share the knowledge that I have about how to prepare for and execute successful negotiations.

I'm always available to answer questions and I can be reached at:

Dr. Jim Anderson
Blue Elephant Consulting
Email: jim@BlueElephantConsulting.com
Facebook: http://goo.gl/1TVoK
Web: **www.BlueElephantConsulting.com**

"Unforgettable communication skills that will set your ideas free…"

Create An Effective Negotiating Team At Your Company!

Dr. Jim Anderson is available to provide training and coaching on the topics that are the most important to people who have to negotiate: how can my team effectively prepare for and execute a successful negotiation that will get us what we both want and need?

Dr. Anderson believes that in order to both learn and remember what he says, audiences need to laugh. Each one of his speeches is full of fun and humor so that what he says "sticks" with everyone.

Dr. Anderson's Negotiating Training Includes:

1. How to plan for a negotiation: what information do you need and where can you find it?

2. What's the best way to explore how a deal can be created during a negotiation?

3. How can you bring a negotiation to a close without giving in to the other side?

Dr. Jim Anderson works with over 100 customers per year. To invite Dr. Anderson to work with you, contact him at:

Phone: 813-418-6970 or
Email: jim@BlueElephantConsulting.com

Blue
Elephant
Consulting

Speaking   Negotiating   Managing   Marketi

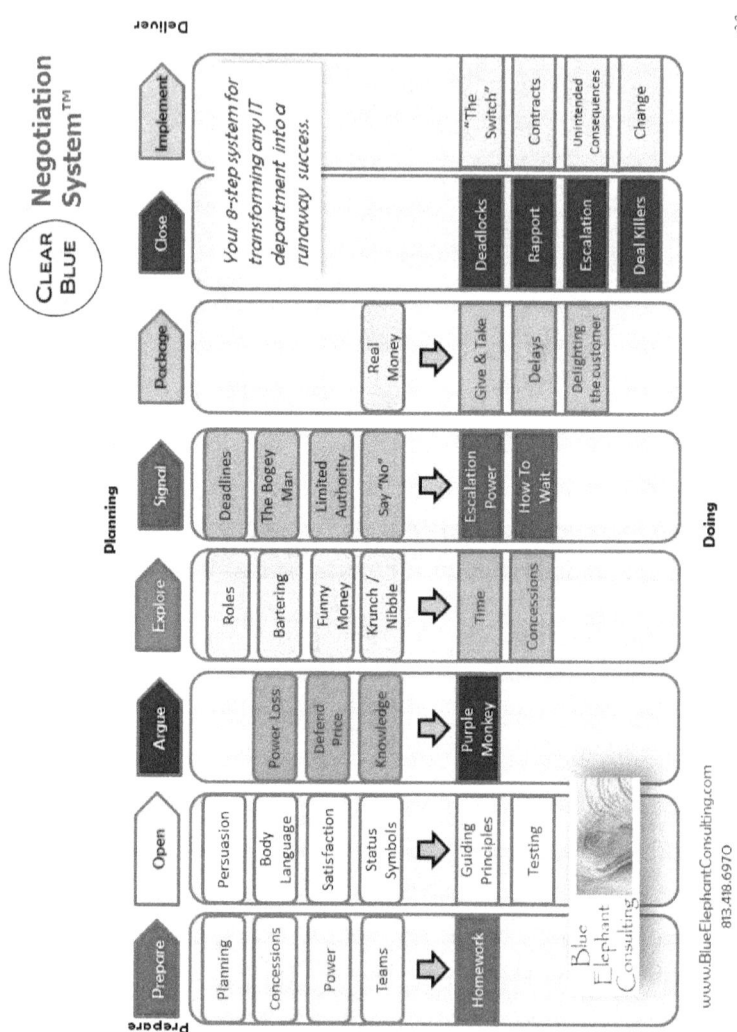

The **Clear Blue Negotiation System™** has been created to provide negotiators with a clear roadmap for how to manage a successful negotiation. This system shows negotiators what needs to be done and in what order to do it.

Chapter 1

A Negotiator's Best Friend: Time To Think

Chapter 1: A Negotiator's Best Friend: Time To Think

Quick – what is the most important characteristic of a negotiator? Sorry, that was a trick question – there are a number of correct possible answers. However, one trait that needs to be on that list is patience. Although being an American can often be a great asset, in negotiations sometimes it can be a hindrance because we are impatient!

So what is patience? In short it's the ability to wait, the ability to not rush to a conclusion. Although this can be very difficult to do, it is a trait well worth developing. With patience you can cause the following things to happen:

1. Get the other side to grant concession after concession.
2. Discover new issues that need to be negotiated.
3. Cause the other side to have internal divisions.
4. Cause the other side to redefine their objectives.
5. Provide time for both sides to accept new ideas.

So if we can all agree that patience is a good thing for a negotiator to have, the big question that comes up right off the bat is just how does one develop patience? Since pressure and patience are so closely linked, the ability to develop patience often comes down to how your organization works.

In order to build patience, here is what you need to do:

1. You need to make sure that you have made sure that everyone on you negotiating team is made aware of the value of patience.

2. You need to take the time to plan ahead.

3. Get an inch, when you really need a yard. Time is something that you can always use – buy yourself more whenever you have an opportunity.

4. Establish milestones that are future based so that everyone has the same view of the future.

5. Manage the expectations of upper management so that pressure on the negotiating team is minimized as much as possible.

Speaking of upper management, as with all negotiating tactics, patience has two sides to it. Your upper management will be well aware that too much patience may result in the negotiating never reaching a conclusion.

Given the way the world works, there is a good chance that you'll encounter a situation in which the other side of the table starts to use patience as a tactic against you! In these situations, there are several ways to defend yourself:

1. Internally understand that his using patience may turn out to make things tougher on the other side than on you.

2. Set a deadline in order to negate the other side's use of patience.

3. React by making sure that you are relaxed and make yourself comfortable.

4. Prepare your internal team for a long march (also make sure that your senior management does not expect immediate results).

5. Develop a strategy that will send signals to the other side that lets them know that patience won't work out

for them.

6.   Make patience both costly and risky for the other side.

7.   Walk out!

Using simple patience is a tactic that is often overlooked in today's go-go business environment. That's one of the reasons that it can work so well! Make sure that you communicate the importance of patience to your entire negotiating team and you'll be well positioned to do well during your next negotiation.

Chapter 2

A Sales Negotiator's Friend: "Just The Facts, M'am"

Chapter 2: A Sales Negotiator's Friend: "Just The Facts, M'am"

So there you are, getting ready to fire up your side of a sales deal when all of a sudden you get hit with a volley of facts, averages, and statistics. You're hit! Each one of those figures came with a sharp point that has embedded itself, perhaps fatally, into your arguments. Is there any way that you can survive?

Good news, the answer is yes. It turns out that these powerful negotiating weapons: facts, averages, and statistics are ALWAYS negotiable. We have trial lawyers to thank for showing us the way. The key here is not to argue with the numbers themselves, but rather dispute what lies behind the numbers.

Questions that a good salesperson will ask right off the bat after being attacked with numbers include:

1. Who collected these numbers?

2. What sources did they use to get the numbers?

3. What techniques did they use to collect the numbers?

4. Were there any assumptions used when collecting the numbers?

5. Why were the numbers collected in the first place?

6. What values were hidden behind the numbers?

7. Were there any biases that might have influenced the collection?

A key point to always remember is that any facts, statistics, or averages are always based on things that have happened in the past. What you are in the process of trying to do is to negotiate a deal that will live in the future.

One final point is to not allow yourself to get too worried by statistics or averages. They are just ways of trying to be able to talk about large amounts of data. The most important thing to remember here is that by their very definition, statistics and averages really don't apply to anyone including you.

Chapter 3

Giving To Get: How A Sales Negotiator Makes Concessions

Chapter 3: Giving To Get: How A Sales Negotiator Makes Concessions

Sales negotiating is all about concessions. You make them, the other side makes them. Finally, if enough has been given, then you should be able to reach a common middle ground where a deal can be struck.

The trick is knowing how and when you should make your concessions. Here are some tips from the pros to make sure that you do it correctly:

1. **Plenty of Room**: Make sure that you always give yourself plenty of room to negotiate. Simple things like starting with a high price or a lengthy delivery cycle will buy you the room to make concessions during the negotiations.

2. **Hide Your Cards**: You always want to work to make the other side of the table open up and put all of his cards on the table long before you have to do the same. You should keep your motivations and goals hidden from view in order to maintain your negotiating power.

3. **Be Second**: Never make a major concession first. Once again this is a power thing. Instead, make minor concessions until the cows come home.

4. **Make 'Em Earn It**: Never make a concession without making the other side earn it first. If they don't earn it, then they won't appreciate the concession when you give it to them.

5. **Wait**: Make sure that you hold on to your concessions for as long as you can. Giving in later in the negotiation is always better than earlier – and the other side will

appreciate it more (see #4).

6. **No Tit-For-Tat**: it turns out that tit-for-tat or one-for-one concessions are not necessary. It's ok if the other side gives more than you do.

7. **Gimme**: Make sure that you get something for every concession that you make.

8. **Empty Boxes**: Give concessions that really give nothing away from your point of view.

9. **Words**: Getting the other side to say "I'll consider it" is one form of a concession.

10. **Promises**: Just like in #9, getting the other side to make a promise is yet another form of having them make a concession.

Chapter 4

Even More Giving: 5 More Ways Sales Negotiators Can Use Concessions

Chapter 4: Even More Giving: 5 More Ways Sales Negotiators Can Use Concessions

You can never say it too many times: in order to reach an agreement with the other side during a sales negotiation, you **ALWAYS** have to make some sort of concession(s). The trick to doing this correctly is to make sure that you don't make so many concessions that when a deal is struck that you're left feeling that you didn't get a good deal.

Once upon a time I was in the process of moving to start a new job and had to sell my house. I had found an interested buyer and we were in the processing of negotiating a selling price. We had gotten pretty close to an agreement, but we were not quite there.

I knew that all of the appliances in the house were pretty much on their last legs, and I was concerned that the buyer was going to ask me to replace them as a part of the deal. I had already moved so that would have been a big inconvenience to contract out the work, oversee it, and pay for it. However, the buyer only came back and asked me to **replace the hot water heaters**. I negotiated just paying him cash to have him take care of it and then we were able to strike a deal.

[Editors Note: I later found out that he pocketed the cash that I gave him, didn't fix the hot water heaters which were in the attic, and shortly thereafter **they failed and flooded the house**. Ouch – there's a lesson in there somewhere]

Here are few additional guidelines on how to make concessions work for you during your next sales negotiation:

1. Try to not negotiate using so-called **"funny money"** – taxes, credit cards, monthly payments, and interest

rates. Stick to the real stuff that everyone understands.

2. Understand and use the power of the word **"no"**. All too many sales negotiators are afraid to use this word. If you use it over and over again, eventually the other side will come to believe that you really mean it. Persistence pays!

3. In the heat of a sales negotiation, it can be easy to lose track of **what really matters to you**. Make sure that you keep a list of what's important to you (and what's important to the other side) and look at it often.

4. If you make a concession that you later on decide was a bad idea, have the courage to **step back from that concession**. Remember that until the sale is signed for, everything can be re-negotiated. Not stepping back from a previous concession because of pride is one of the biggest mistakes that you can make.

5. **Throttle the other side's expectations**. You are in charge of how many concessions you make and how fast you make them. If you give too much away too soon, then the other side will start to expect even more.

Chapter 5

A Sales Negotiator's Friend: The Telephone

Chapter 5: A Sales Negotiator's Friend: The Telephone

What's your mental picture of a typical sales negotiation? When you close your eyes do you see a lushly carpeted **board room** with a large oval table in the center and padded leather chairs all around it? If so, then in most cases you are sadly mistaken.

An amazing number of sales negotiations occur **over the telephone**. Everyone has one and in fact in this day and age of mobile phones we all seem to have more than one phone. Given that by using the phone you can reach someone directly at almost any time, phones have become an important tool in negotiating sales.

However, as with any tool, a phone can be a **danger** to any negotiator's hope of success. Using a phone to negotiate can be quick and easy, but that's actually part of the problem. I'm not telling you to not use the phone, I'm just saying that you need to watch out when you do. Here are some of the **things that can go wrong** when you use the phone to negotiate a sale:

1. **Deal / No Deal**: Because you can't look the other side in the eye when you are negotiating with them on the phone, it's entirely possible that you may conclude the call thinking that you have a deal when you really don't.

2. **Can You Hear Me Now?** What you think that you are saying is not necessarily what the other side is hearing. However, since you are on a phone, there is no way for you to realize that they have gotten the wrong message.

3. **What Did You Say?** Often when we are negotiating on the phone, we are out and about. Although we may reach agreement, it won't count until such time as we

write it down. That may be hours later and what we write down may be different from what we agreed to.

Once again, the phone is a powerful sales negotiation tool; however, you have to be careful how you use it in order to make sure that you don't get burned.

Chapter 6

---

3 Things Every Sales Negotiator Needs To Know

Chapter 6: 3 Things Every Sales Negotiator Needs To Know

Wouldn't it be great if the best sales negotiators in the world could drop by our place and sit down with us for a while to **share what they've learned**? If you knew that they were coming, what questions would you ask them?

We've already talked about some of the things that master sales negotiators could teach us, and we've covered some of the secrets that they use to walk away with the results that they wanted.

However, let's dive deeper – if we only had a few minutes to talk with a master sales negotiator, **what would they want to share with us**?

Buyers Need To Move Slower Than Sellers

Our sales negotiations are more often than not a game of back-and-forth: offers are followed by counteroffers which are then themselves countered. One thing that too many of us overlook is that the buyer's first counter offer is **one of the most important events** in a sales negotiation.

Before the buyer makes a counteroffer, the buyer has no idea if there is any chance of striking a deal. The more the buyer goes on talking and doesn't make a counteroffer, **the greater the doubt in the seller** will be. In fact, he/she may end up lowering their price just to get the buyer to make a counteroffer in the first place.

Learn To Say "Yes" Slooooowly

Sometimes, no matter what side of the table you are on, you'll be presented with a deal that is perfect just the way it stands. The price is right, the terms are good, and it meets your schedule. You are busy and have lots of other things to do – you want to say "**yes**" and move on to other things.

However, the master sales negotiators would caution you against doing this. It's not that there is anything wrong with the deal, it's just that you are going to leave the other side with **a bad feeling** about the negotiation. They are forever going to be filled with doubts about the deal (and they may do a poor job of keeping their part of the deal). However, if you say "no" a few times or at least take you time saying "yes", then they will feel as though they "**earned**" the final outcome and this will, surprisingly, leave them feeling more satisfied.

Breakdowns – Good For Buyers, Bad For Sellers

Most of the time, the deal that we're negotiating can be quite complex. In these cases it's natural for the buyer to request a **breakdown of the prices** involved. This is an excellent way to get some insight into the seller's costs.

On the other hand, providing such information is going to allow a buyer to do a better job of negotiating a lower price so sellers should work hard to **not have to provide them**. This can be impossible if they ask for it at point blank; however, trying to avoid ever getting into that situation is always a good plan.

Final Thoughts

As we've said before, the art of good sales negotiating does not rely on one single skill. Rather there are literally 1,000s of small details that if you can get them right, then you'll turn into a force to be reckoned with during any sales negotiation. The **three skills** that we've discussed here will get you on your way to becoming a sales negotiating pro and will allow you to close better deals and close them quicker.

Chapter 7

Don't Believe What Anyone Says Is What Sales Negotiators Need To Learn To Do

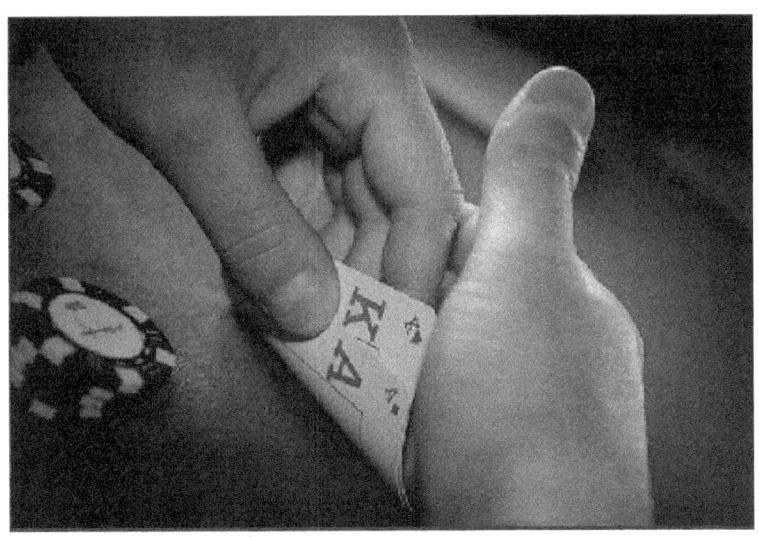

Chapter 7: Don't Believe What Anyone Says Is What Sales Negotiators Need To Learn To Do

People are either honest or they aren't, right? Umm, well not exactly. Look, in a sales negotiation everything is not as it seems. I hate to use strong words like "**lying**" or anything like that, but let's just say that a healthy dose of **skepticism** is often a sales negotiator's best friend.

What's Going On Here – Can't Anyone Tell The Truth?

The older a sales negotiator gets, the more he / she is less likely to believe just about **ANYTHING** that they are told. There is a reason for this! In the end, sales negotiating is all about power – who has it and who doesn't. However, just like in the game of poker **bluffing** is not only allowed, it is often encouraged.

If you don't believe me (or you don't WANT to believe me), then think about how a buyer and a seller interact when they are trying to complete a deal to **buy a house** – talk about some serious poker playing!

Where Do The Lines Get Drawn?

We are in a very murky area here and it's very easy for a sales negotiator to stumble over the line and fall into the **dark side** – becoming a flat-out liar. It's necessary that you operate here, but you've got to watch your step.

Our house buyer / seller are going to be presenting information that may **not quite be the complete truth**. The house seller is going to be talking about all of the things that make the house a fantastic house – and leaving out any discussion about the leaky pipes in the basement and the squirrels that have set up a home in the attic.

Likewise the buyer is going to be trying to mask any real interest that he / she may have in buying this particular house. Additionally, the buyer will be working hard to NOT communicate how much funding he / she has to complete the purchase. Is anyone lying here? No – but they are also not telling the **complete truth**.

One Word – Be Skeptical

A good sales negotiator is **ALWAYS** skeptical about anything that he / she is told by the other side. This includes when the other side uses facts & figures (where did they come from?), experts (what makes them an expert?), and handsome bound color documents (Kinko's can turn out great stuff overnight).

As a sales negotiator your job is to always be **asking questions**. Take nothing at face value and always assume that the other side is probably not giving you the complete story. This is how you are going to transfer power from the other side to you.

Final Thoughts

Being a "**doubting Thomas**" is a great skill for a sales negotiator to have. One important rule of life has been given to us by the Las Vegas board of tourism: "What happens during a Sales Negotiation, **stays in the negotiation**." This means that you can't have any hard feelings about what information the other side revealed (or didn't) during the negotiation after it is all over and done. Having a healthy dose of doubt while negotiating will allow you to close better deals and close them quicker.

Chapter 8

Sales Negotiation Tips From Brian Dietmeyer

Chapter 8: Sales Negotiation Tips From Brian Dietmeyer

The basics of sales negotiations are pretty straightforward; however, it can be easy to lose sight of them as we talk about tactics, preparation, and detailed sales negotiation skills. Maybe it's time that we took a step back and got an expert to remind us about what we really need to be doing in our next sales negotiation?

Introducing Brian Dietmeyer

Brian Dietmeyer is the President / CEO of a company called Think! that offers business-to-business negotiation training. He's also written a book called **Strategic Negotiation: A Breakthrough Four-Step Process for Effective Business Negotiation.**

A while ago Brian sat down with the folks over at SellingPower magazine and went over the fundamental things that we all have to remember when we start a sales negotiation. He does a pretty good job of hitting most of the bases.

Brian's Negotiating Tips

Brian believes that when it comes time to start a negotiation, we can anticipate roughly 80% of what will happen during the negotiation. Brian believes that that we are wasting our time when we try to prepare for every possible event that might occur – we already know what will probably happen.

Brian believes that for every negotiation there are two questions that you need to identify the answers to before the negotiation starts. The first question is what will both parties do if you are not able to reach an agreement? The second question is what will the likely terms of the deal be if you are able to reach an agreement? Using the answers to these two questions will allow you to blueprint your negotiation.

Brian believes that we need to start our negotiation by focusing on the CNA (Consequence of No Agreement) for both sides. One or more sides will probably be talking about the deal that they can get from someone else – this is one form of their CNA.

Every negotiation is made up of a number of different issues. Brian understands that we can sometimes spend too much time focused on a single issue, such as price. What he recommends that we do is to make sure that all of the issues that are being discussed remain on the table in front of everyone so that they can be seen.

In order to be able to reach the deal that you want in a negotiation, you need to have taken the time to collect all of the information that you can get about CNAs for both sides and other aspects of this negotiation. One of the most important things that you'll need to have information on will be the other side's alternatives. Before they bring them up, you need to fully understand what would happen if they selected them.

Chapter 9

Haggling Is Becoming A Part Of Every Sales Deal

Chapter 9: Haggling Is Becoming A Part Of Every Sales Deal

Welcome to the new world order: **consumers are learning to haggle**. In the extended global economic recession, consumers who never used to even think about bargaining are suddenly starting to haggle over every deal. Is this a good thing or a bad thing?

As you might expect, haggling has arrived first at the firms that have been the hardest hit by the recession. This includes the hotel business as well as clothes and electronics stores. All three of these firms are very interested in **moving merchandise as quickly as possible**. That's why they are now open to making deals with their customers.

The market research firm America's Research Group has just completed a study that shows that **72%** of American consumers reported that they had haggled in the past four months. This is up from **56%** just a year ago. What's really telling is that the same consumers report that they have been successful in getting a better deal **80%** of the time.

Different Approaches Seem To Be Working

Consumers are discovering that negotiating for a better deal seems to work with **just about any business transaction**. Formerly off-limits firms including the New York Plaza hotel and Nordstrom are starting to warm to the idea of having their customers bargain with them for the best deal.

Customers are finding that they may not always be able to get a discount on an item that they are interested in buying. However, getting the seller to cover shipping or the sales tax seems to work. If that fails, then having the seller **include an**

additional item in order to complete the deal has also proven to be successful.

Secrets To Successful Haggling

Many firms are creating programs to deal with consumers who want a better deal. However, in order to protect their margins, they are **not advertising** these programs – they only offer them when the consumer pushes them.

Credit card companies are notorious for doing this. They are willing to negotiate on interest rates and late fees. However, the only way customers can find out where the companies are flexible is **by asking**.

Final Thoughts

The arrival of the new style of haggling for better deals is showing up in the **hardest hit industries**: cars, real estate, etc. However, we should expect this to spread quickly to other industries.

The big question will be whether or not this marks a **fundamental change** in how consumers go shopping: are they going to expect to have to bargain for everything in the future? No matter what the answer is, in the short term this type of sales negotiating is bound to boost sales. Sales negotiators who learn how to take advantage of this new style of buying will be able to close better deals and close them quicker.

Chapter 10

Hidden Needs Drive Sales Negotiations

Chapter 10: Hidden Needs Drive Sales Negotiations

All sales negotiations are driven by both public and private needs. If you can understand and deal with the other side's **hidden needs**, then you'll have more power during the negotiation.

It's What Lies Below The Surface That Really Matters

When we enter into a sales negotiation, we like to kid ourselves that we know what the other side is looking to get out of the negotiation. At least **on the surface**, all sales negotiations look the same.

The easy-to-see desires of the other side generally come down to one of three things: **money, goods, and / or services**. This is what we can see and this is what we spend our time preparing to negotiate. However, that's really only part of the story.

Knowledge Of Hidden Needs Boosts Your Power

I'm sure that you're probably already agreeing with me that knowing the other side of the table's hidden needs would be advantageous when you are getting ready to negotiate. However, did you know that this knowledge will increase your **negotiating power**?

Remember that power in a sales negotiation is a difficult thing to nail down. However, the more that you know about the other side and their hidden needs, then the **more negotiating power** you'll have.

The Search For Hidden Needs

If we can all agree that identifying the other side's hidden needs is a good thing, than all that is left for us to talk about is just exactly **HOW** you can go about doing that. The key is to have a good set of questions.

These are the questions that you need to ask yourself **BEFORE** you enter into a sales negotiation. Not every question will pertain to this specific negotiation and your list will evolve over time. Here's a good set of questions for you to start asking yourself:

1. Do they want to make their lives easier?
2. Do they want to appear to be competent?
3. Do they want peace of mind?
4. Do they want to be listened to?
5. Do they want freedom of choice?
6. Do they want to keep their job?
7. Do they want recognition?
8. Do they want to be liked?

Final Thoughts

As you enter into a sales negotiation, you need to realize that the other side of the table probably has more hidden needs than they have publicly known needs. What this means for you is that the other side of the table won't say "yes" to your requests until after at least some of their hidden wants **have been fulfilled**.

In the end, all negotiating is about making sure that you have enough power to be successful. One of the most important keys is to realize that we need to also **address the other side of the table's hidden needs** in order reach an agreement that both sides can live with.

If you can learn to spot these hidden needs before you enter into your next negotiation, then you will be able to close **better deals** and close them **quicker**.

Chapter 11

Negotiators Know That Persistence (& Risk Taking) Pay Off

Chapter 11: Negotiators Know That Persistence (& Risk Taking) Pay Off

In this world there are two types of negotiators: the good ones and everyone else. The goal of any negotiator is to become a member of the group of good negotiators. The challenge is that the path to becoming a good negotiator is not always clear. However, there are **two basic skills** that lay on this path: persistence and the ability to take the right risks.

Persistence Pays Off For Negotiators

Persistence is another one of those skills that we all think should be obvious to ever negotiator; however, it's very easy to not have it. When the other side of the table says "**no**" to one of our offers during a negotiation, it's very easy to lose heart and **give up**.

However, the negotiator who treats every "no" as a step towards "**yes**" is the one who will be successful in the end. Realizing that there is a reason that the other side is saying no and then being **persistent enough** to continue talking until you uncover that reason is the key to success.

American negotiators have been confronted with negotiators from other countries who appeared to be **unmovable** in their positions. Day after day the negotiations would continue with no progress being made. In the case where the Americans would return to the table and not give up, eventually progress ended up being made. The other side's unmovable position was just a ploy to see **how committed** the Americans were to the negotiations.

Risk Taking Has Its Rewards

Being persistent in a negotiation is a form of risk taking: you are risking continuing down a path that may not pan out for you. However, there are **other forms of risk taking** that can occur during a negotiation:

Deadlock: The risk of encountering a deadlock faces every negotiator. The more you press a point, the greater the possibility that the other side will become unyielding. A skilled negotiator knows how to not force the other side into a position from which there is no way out.

Losing Current Deals: Whenever a change to an existing deal is being negotiated, both parties realize that there is a risk that they could walk away from the table with no deal at all. Often it's this fear of losing an existing deal that will keep both parties at the table. Sharp negotiators realize this and will be willing to push harder because they know the other side of the table won't walk away.

Losing Opportunities: Both buyers and sellers can potentially not realize that a deal is more important to the other side than it seems at first glance. Sellers may be trying to break into a new market or buyers may be trying to get additional suppliers. In situations like this, the other side of the table can press harder because the risk of reaching a deadlock is much less.

Final Thoughts

Successful negotiators aren't that much different from everyone else. The things that distinguish them are actually **very small details**. Two of the most important features of a good negotiator are persistence and knowing when to take risks.

Persistence means knowing when to keep on even after you've been told "no" by the other side. Good risk taking is when you know that your persistence will pay off for you in the end. When you can **combine these skills**, you will have become a good negotiator and you will be able to close **better deals** and close them **quicker**.

Chapter 12

How To Win A Race When You're Not The Fastest Runner

Chapter 12: How To Win A Race When You're Not The Fastest Runner

Sales negotiators are often our own worst enemies. So much of what it takes to have a successful negotiation depends on **your mental state** going into the negotiation that if you don't believe that you can close this deal, then I've got some bad news for you – you probably won't.

One situation that my students seem to struggle with over and over again is the case where it's them and a whole bunch of other companies **all trying to get the same deal**. The other companies appear to be prettier, smarter, and all around better: what chance do any of us have against them?

The Many Going After One Challenge

This is arguably the classic negotiating challenge. We see this all the time in real life when we want to buy a house that someone else also wants to buy or we want something on eBay that lots of other people want (and are willing to pay more to get). When the other side of the table is a single party and our side of the table is packed with us and our competitors, it can get to be a little bit **disheartening**.

The thing that I tell my students to remember is that things are never as they look. When you are in a highly competitive situation, it's all too easy to look around and start to **lose hope** because you see how many other people want the same thing that you do: there can only be one winner. What you are missing here is that no matter how shiny they all look on the outside, the number of parties that you are actually competing against is really very small.

Why You Actually Have A Good Chance Of Winning The Deal

So here's the deal. When you are going after a deal and there are a lot of other firms doing the same thing, you should not worry too much about them. The reason is that despite their numbers, the actual number of firms that you'll be competing against is **relatively small**. Here's why:

1. People at the other side of the table may not like a firm for some reason and so their offer won't be considered.

2. A firm's past history with the other side of the table (missed deliveries, poor quality, etc.) may make its offer be rejected.

3. Size of the firm: perhaps it's too big for the job or maybe it's too small to pull it off.

4. Product Features: many times a competitor's solution may do more than yours, but the other side of the tale doesn't value those features so their price will be too high.

5. No pricing: amazingly enough, sometimes a firm won't be able to get through all of its internal hoops in time to be able to deliver a price.

6. Unknown firm: if the other side of the table doesn't know a firm, that is have an existing relationship with them, then they may reject doing business with them.

7. Financial trouble: some competitors may be having money troubles that mean that nobody is going to risk doing business with them.

Final Thoughts

Having the **confidence** that you'll be able to close a deal is critical to being a successful negotiator. Often it will be you against the world as you attempt to be the one that the other side of the table selects. In these cases it can be all too easy to lose heart, the other firms may look as though they are better positioned to win than you are.

However, you've got to realize that **appearances can be deceiving**. Many of the other firms will fall by the wayside for one or more reasons that may not be obvious to you. Once you realize this, you should become more confidant in your ability to strike a deal.

Having this knowledge will prevent you from automatically providing concessions to the other side during your negotiations. **These concessions may not be needed** because much of the competition will not truly be considered. Once you know this, you should be able to strike better deals and do it quicker.

It's from the forge of failure that the steel of success is formed.

Hard Work Does Not Guarantee Success, But Success Does Not Happen Without Hard Work.

- Dr. Jim Anderson

Create An Effective Negotiating Team At Your Company!

Dr. Jim Anderson is available to provide training and coaching on the topics that are the most important to people who have to negotiate: how can my team effectively prepare for and execute a successful negotiation that will get us what we both want and need?

Dr. Anderson believes that in order to both learn and remember what he says, audiences need to laugh. Each one of his speeches is full of fun and humor so that what he says "sticks" with everyone.

Dr. Anderson's Negotiating Training Includes:

1. How to plan for a negotiation: what information do you need and where can you find it?

2. What's the best way to explore how a deal can be created during a negotiation?

3. How can you bring a negotiation to a close without giving in to the other side?

Dr. Jim Anderson works with over 100 customers per year. To invite Dr. Anderson to work with you, contact him at:

Phone: 813-418-6970 or
Email: jim@BlueElephantConsulting.com

Photo Credits:

Chapter 8 - Blog Talk Radio
http://www.blogtalkradio.com/waynehurlbert/2012/11/30/brian-dietmeyer-poet-and-warrior

Chapter 9 – Pimthida
https://www.flickr.com/photos/pimthida/

Chapter 10 – Bruce
https://www.flickr.com/photos/67114894@N00/

Chapter 11 - Tiago Daniel
https://www.flickr.com/photos/bazik/

Chapter 12 - Steven Pisano
https://www.flickr.com/photos/stevenpisano/

Other Books By
The Author

Product Management

- How Product Managers Can Sell More Of Their Product: Tips & Techniques For Product Managers To Better Understand How To Sell Their Product

- How To Create A Successful Product That Customers Will Want: Techniques For Product Managers To Boost Product Sales And Increase Customer Satisfaction

- What Product Managers Need To Know About World-Class Product Development: How Product Managers Can Create Successful Products

- How Product Managers Can Learn To Understand Their Customers: Techniques For Product Managers To Better Understand What Their Customers Really Want

- Product Management Secrets: Techniques For Product Managers To Boost Product Sales And Increase Customer Satisfaction

- Product Development Lessons For Product Managers: How Product Managers Can Create Successful Products

- Customer Lessons For Product Managers: Techniques For Product Managers To Better Understand What Their Customers Really Want

- Product Failure Lessons For Product Managers: Examples Of Products That Have Failed For Product Managers To Learn From

- Communication Skills For Product Managers: The Communication Skills That Product Managers Need To Know How To Use In Order To Have A Successful Product

- How To Have A Successful Product Manager Career: The Things That You Need To Be Doing TODAY In Order To Have A Successful Product Manager Career

- Product Manager Product Success: How to keep your product on track and make it become a success

Public Speaking

- Changing How You Speak To Overcome Your Fear Of Speaking: Change techniques that will transform a speech into a memorable event

- Delivering Excellence: How To Give Presentations That Make A Difference: Presentation techniques that will transform a speech into a memorable event

- Tools Speakers Need In Order To Give The Perfect Speech: What tools to use to create your next speech so that your message will be remembered forever!

- How To Create A Speech That Will Be Remembered

- Secrets To Organizing A Speech For Maximum Impact: How to put together a speech that will capture and hold your audience's attention

- How To Become A Better Speaker By Changing How You Speak: Change techniques that will transform a speech into a memorable event

- How To Give A Great Presentation: Presentation techniques that will transform a speech into a memorable event

- How To Rehearse In Order To Give The Perfect Speech: How to effectively rehearse your next speech to that your message be remembered forever!

- Secrets To Creating The Perfect Speech: How to create a speech that will make your message be remembered forever!

- Secrets To Organizing The Perfect Speech: How to organize the best speech of your life!

- Secrets To Planning The Perfect Speech: How to plan to give the best speech of your life

- How To Show What You Mean During A Presentation: How to use visual techniques to transform a speech into a memorable event

CIO Skills

- Keeping The Barbarians Out: How CIOs Can Secure Their Department and Company: Tips And Techniques For CIOs To Use In Order To Secure Both Their IT Department And Their Company

- What CIOs Need To Know In Order To Successfully Manage An IT Department: Decision Making Skills That Every CIO Needs To Have In Order To Be Able

To Make The Right Choices

- Becoming A Powerful And Effective Leader: Tips And Techniques That IT Managers Can Use In Order To Develop Leadership Skills

- CIO Secrets For Growing Innovation: Tips And Techniques For CIOs To Use In Order To Make Innovation Happen In Their IT Department

- Your Success As A CIO Depends On How Well You Communicate: Tips And Techniques For CIOs To Use In Order To Become Better Communicators

- What CIOs Need To Know About Working With Partners: Techniques For CIOs To Use In Order To Be Able To Successfully Work With Partners

- Critical CIO Management Skills: Decision Making Skills That Every CIO Needs To Have In Order To Be Able To Make The Right Choices

- How CIOs Can Make Innovation Happen: Tips And Techniques For CIOs To Use In Order To Make Innovation Happen In Their IT Department

- CIO Communication Skills Secrets: Tips And Techniques For CIOs To Use In Order To Become

Better Communicators

- Managing Your CIO Career: Steps That CIOs Have To Take In Order To Have A Long And Successful Career

- CIO Business Skills: How CIOs can work effectively with the rest of the company!

IT Manager Skills

- How To Build High Performance IT Teams: Tips And Techniques That IT Managers Can Use In Order To Develop Productive Teams

- Save Yourself, Save Your Job – How To Manage Your IT Career: Secrets That IT Managers Can Use In Order To Have A Successful Career

- Growing Your CIO Career: How CIOs Can Work With The Entire Company In Order To Be Successful

- How IT Managers Can Make Innovation Happen: Tips And Techniques For IT Managers To Use In Order To Make Innovation Happen In Their Teams

- Staffing Skills IT Managers Must Have: Tips And Techniques That IT Managers Can Use In Order To

Correctly Staff Their Teams

- Secrets Of Effective Leadership For IT Managers: Tips And Techniques That IT Managers Can Use In Order To Develop Leadership Skills

- IT Manager Career Secrets: Tips And Techniques That IT Managers Can Use In Order To Have A Successful Career

- IT Manager Budgeting Skills: How IT Managers Can Request, Manage, Use, And Track Their Funding

- Secrets Of Managing Budgets: What IT Managers Need To Know In Order To Understand How Their Company Uses Money

Negotiating

- Use The Power Of Arguing To Win Your Next Negotiation: How To Develop The Skill Of Effective Arguing In A Negotiation In Order To Get The Best Possible Outcome

- Learn How To Signal In Your Next Negotiation: How To Develop The Skill Of Effective Signaling In A Negotiation In Order To Get The Best Possible Outcome

- Learn The Skill Of Exploring In A Negotiation: How To Develop The Skill Of Exploring What Is Possible In A Negotiation In Order To Reach The Best Possible Deal

- Learn How To Argue In Your Next Negotiation: How To Develop The Skill Of Effective Arguing In A Negotiation In Order To Get The Best Possible Outcome|

- How To Open Your Next Negotiation: How To Start A Negotiation In Order To Get The Best Possible Outcome

- Preparing For Your Next Negotiation: What You Need To Do BEFORE A Negotiation Starts In Order To Get The Best Possible Deal

- Learn How To Package Trades In Your Next Negotiation

- All Good Things Come To An End: How To Close A Negotiation - How To Develop The Skill Of Closing In Order To Get The Best Possible Outcome From A Negotiation

- Take No Prisoners In Your Next Negotiation: How To Start A Negotiation In Order To Get The Best

Possible Outcome

Miscellaneous

- How To Heal A Broken Leg – Fast!: Understanding how to deal with a broken leg in order to start walking again quickly

- How Software Defined Networking (SDN) Is Going To Change Your World Forever: The Revolution In Network Design And How It Affects You

- The Power Of Virtualization: How It Affects Memory, Servers, and Storage: The Revolution In Creating Virtual Devices And How It Affects You

- The Internet-Enabled Successful School District Superintendent: How To Use The Internet To Boost Parental Involvement In Your Schools

- Power Distribution Unit (PDU) Secrets: What Everyone Who Works In A Data Center Needs To Know!

- Making The Jump: How To Land Your Dream Job When You Get Out Of College!

- How To Use The Internet To Create Successful Students And Involved Parents

How To Develop The Skill Of Exploring What Is Possible In A Negotiation In Order To Reach The Best Possible Deal

This book has been written with one goal in mind – to show you how to use the skill of exploring in your next negotiation. It's not easy being a negotiator and so we're going to show you how to get the information that you need in order to get the deal that you want!

Let's Make Your Negotiation A Success!

What You'll Find Inside:

- **GIVING TO GET: HOW A SALES NEGOTIATOR MAKES CONCESSIONS**

- **3 THINGS EVERY SALES NEGOTIATOR NEEDS TO KNOW**

- **HIDDEN NEEDS DRIVE SALES NEGOTIATIONS**

- **HOW TO WIN A RACE WHEN YOU'RE NOT THE FASTEST RUNNER**

Dr. Jim Anderson brings his 25 years of real-world experience to this book. He's been a negotiator at some of the world's largest firms. He's going to show you what you need to do (and not do!) in order to get the best deal out of your next negotiation!

www.ingramcontent.com/pod-product-compliance
Lightning Source LLC
Chambersburg PA
CBHW061205180526
45170CB00002B/973